IT'S THE LA

WRITTEN BY
CHRISTOPHER YEATES

COVER AND ILLUSTRATIONS BY
ZOE SADLER

© Gresham Books 2016
Published by Gresham Books Limited
The Carriage House, Ningwood Manor, Ningwood,
Isle of Wight PO30 4NJ
ISBN 978 0 946095 75 9

WHAT'S INSIDE

BRITISH VALUES

Britain is made up of England, Wales and Scotland, and the people who live in these countries are called **British**. The people of Northern Ireland may also call themselves British and together we make up the **United Kingdom**. This book is to help you learn about and come to understand some of the British Values we all share.

WHY DO WE NEED RULES?

You probably have rules at home about bedtimes and homework. You definitely have rules at school.

But what are all these rules for? Why do we need them?

➜ Rules help keep you and your things safe.
➜ Rules make sure that everybody is treated fairly. Being fair means that everybody is treated in the same way.
➜ Rules help keep things organised. Think of the rules you have when you play a game. If there were no rules the game would not work.

Rules exist to make your life better. Living in a world which is safe, fair and organised is far more likely to make us happy than living in one which is dangerous, unfair and chaotic.

What we mean when we say...

Fair: treating people in the same way without favouritism.

Chaotic: disorganised.

Your turn to speak

→ Discuss with your talking partner some of the rules you have at school and decide whether or not these rules make your lives safer, fairer and more organised.

Read and understand

1. You probably have lots of rules at home to help keep you safe, for example, looking both ways when you cross the road. Make a list of rules that help keep you safe.

2. Make a list of the rules you have at school that you think help you the most, for example, rules about sharing or listening to other people.

3. Ask your teacher which three rules are most important to them and draw a picture showing how each one helps you and your class.

4. Write a paragraph explaining why we have rules.

BEING RESPONSIBLE FOR YOUR OWN ACTIONS

Getting into trouble because you have broken a rule can be scary. But it is important that rules are obeyed, and it is right that you should know what will happen if you *do* break the rules. This is because we are all responsible for our own behaviour.

Being responsible means that it is you, and you alone, who has control over how you treat the people around you, and how you choose to behave.

It is very important to always try to be as fair and respectful as you possibly can. This might mean remembering to share, or wait your turn, or not talk over someone else. If you are fair and respectful towards other people, it is far more likely they will be fair and respectful towards you.

What we mean when we say...

Responsible: being in charge of, or the cause of, something.

Respectful: showing politeness to other people.

Your turn to speak

Make a list with your partner of the types of behaviour that you think are fair and respectful to other people.

Discuss with your partner:

→ How it feels when people don't think about your feelings.

→ Are there any times when you have blamed another person for something you have done wrong?

Read and understand

1. Draw a picture of someone doing something that shows respect to another person. This could be by listening carefully when someone is talking, or waiting patiently for their turn, or sharing.

2. Write about a punishment that has made you think twice about doing something wrong.

3. Explain why you think it is important for us each to be responsible for our own actions.

RULES BEYOND THE CLASSROOM: THE LAW OF THE LAND

Rules that everybody in the whole country must obey are called laws.

The laws that a country has for all its citizens are called the Law of the Land. You could say that laws work very much like school rules, except laws apply to everybody – even the Prime Minister.

Laws work in the same way as rules. Having a strong and fair set of laws that benefits everybody is an important part of living in a democracy. In a democracy, everybody has a voice, and nobody should be treated unfairly because of who they are, where they come from or what they believe. We call this idea equality.

Equality means that everyone should be treated in the same way.

Making things as equal and as fair as possible is an extremely important part of how the law works in this country.

You can find out lots more about democracy in a little book called – 'Let's Vote On It!'

This is Lady Justice, a goddess whose name in Ancient Greece was Themis. She is the referee of the justice system.

You will notice she is wearing a blindfold; this is to make sure the justice she provides is fair to everybody. Lady Justice upholds equality by taking no notice of who is rich or poor, young or old.

In her left hand she holds balance scales, which represent the weighing of evidence. Rather than simply punishing people she doesn't like, or just having a guess at who is guilty, Lady Justice always uses facts, proof and evidence.

Finally, Lady Justice has a sword to show the power and strength of justice.

What we mean when we say...

Law of the Land: rules we all agree to live by so that society runs safely and smoothly. Anybody who breaks the Law of the Land is likely to be punished.

Democracy: a system where the people of a country vote for representatives to run the country.

Equality: where everyone is treated the same and enjoys the same rights and opportunities.

Evidence: facts provided to help prove something is true.

Your turn to speak

Discuss with your partner:

→ Why do you think some people break the law?

→ Why do you think it is important that Lady Justice treats everyone equally?

Read and understand

1. Draw your own picture of Lady Justice wearing her blindfold, and holding her balance scales in her left hand and her sword in her right hand.

2. Explain why Lady Justice is wearing a blindfold and is holding balance scales and a sword.

3. Can you explain what we mean by the Law of the Land?

4. Make a list of some of the laws that you and your family obey.

YOUR VOICE, YOUR LAWS: PARLIAMENT

We all have a voice in deciding the laws of our country. We do this by selecting people to make laws for us. We call this system Parliamentary democracy.

In a Parliamentary democracy, the people who make the laws represent us and make decisions about new laws on our behalf. But they only have the power to do so because we have voted for them in an election.

The people we select to represent us become Members of Parliament and they sit in the House of Commons. We call them MPs. There are 650 MPs, one for each area of the UK. We call each area a constituency.

Elections are the most important part of living in a democracy. This is because elections let everybody aged 18 and over choose (or vote for) those whom they want to represent them. It is just the same idea as when you vote in your own school council elections for people to represent you.

General Elections happen at least once every five years. At a General Election, all the voters in the country choose the MPs they want to represent them in Parliament.

The main job of Parliament is to make the country's laws.

What we mean when we say...

Parliamentary Democracy: a system in which people elect representatives to a Parliament to make laws.

The House of Commons: the democratically elected part of Parliament. It is made up of 650 MPs, one from each constituency. The House of Commons plays the most important role in creating and making laws.

General Election: when the country votes for the representatives who will become Members of Parliament. General Elections happen at least every five years.

Constituency: one of 650 communities of voters within Britain which elect an MP to represent them in Parliament.

MP: Member of Parliament. MPs represent the views of the people in their constituency.

Your turn to speak

Discuss with your partner:

→ What is a Parliamentary democracy?

→ Why do you think it is important that voters get the chance to vote for the people that represent them?

Read and understand

1. Pretend that you want to become a Member of Parliament. Make a poster telling people why they should vote for you.

2. How many Members of Parliament are there in the UK?

3. How old do you need to be to vote in an election?

4. What is the most important job of the House of Commons?

MEET THE JUDGES: THE JUDICIARY

The people who look after the law in the UK are called the judiciary. The main job of the judiciary is to look after our country's legal system – its laws, and how these laws work.

The main way in which the judiciary looks after the legal system is through our law courts. A law court is a place where it is decided who is right and who is wrong, or whether someone is guilty of a crime and how they should be punished.

The court system is run by senior lawyers called judges, who use their knowledge and experience of the law to make sure that justice is upheld.

But what is justice?

Justice basically means fairness.

An important part of the UK's justice system is the idea of individual liberty. As long as you are not breaking the Law of the Land or hurting other people, you are free to act and speak and think however you like.

If you obey the law and respect others, the law will protect you and help you live your life safely and happily.

This girl is breaking the law. Can you explain why?

What we mean when we say...

Law Court: is a place where evidence is put forward to decide who is at fault or has committed a crime.

Legal System: the set of laws of a country, and how they are interpreted, applied and enforced.

Justice: the quality of being fair and reasonable.

Individual Liberty: being free to think, speak and act as you like so long as you don't hurt other people.

Judiciary: the judges who look after the country's legal system, and interpret and apply its laws. They are responsible for upholding justice.

Judge: an important person within the judiciary. A judge is an expert in the law, and upholds justice in the courts.

Your turn to speak

Discuss with your partner:

→ Discuss together how you would explain what justice means. Can you think of any good examples of situations where you can see justice working?

→ Do you think we should all be able to say or do anything we want to? What problems might this cause?

Read and understand

1. Design your own badge or symbol for justice.

2. What is the judiciary?

3. Who runs the court system?

4. Who is the head of the judiciary?

DON'T MESS WITH THE JUDGES: JUDICIAL INDEPENDENCE

Judges help maintain our freedom by being completely fair and objective. Objective means only paying attention to facts and evidence, and not being influenced by personal likes or dislikes.

Lady Justice's blindfold helps her to be objective, because it means she can ignore people who try to influence her.

For judges to be completely fair and objective, it is necessary for them to be independent.

Judicial independence means that no one is allowed to interfere with a judge's decisions. This includes MPs. Politicians can influence the army, they can influence the police, but they are not allowed to influence the decisions of judges.

Judges cannot be prosecuted for anything they say or do while they are busy being a judge. Again, this is to encourage them only to think about what is the most fair and just decision they can make.

What we mean when we say...

Judicial Independence: the idea that the legal system should not be influenced by Parliament or the Government. Lady Justice would not be happy if it were.

Prosecute: take someone to court and accuse them of a crime.

Objective: only paying attention to facts and evidence, and not being influenced by personal likes or dislikes.

Your turn to speak

Discuss with your partner:

→ Can you think of a time when you have been asked to decide who is right in an argument? Explain to your partner how sticking to the facts might help you decide who is right and who is wrong.

→ Why do you think someone might try to influence a judge's decisions?

→ Why is it important for judges only to be guided by facts and evidence (and not by their personal likes or dislikes)?

Read and understand

1. Draw a picture of a judge deciding who is right and who is wrong. Draw all the people who might be trying to influence the judge in their decision.

2. Explain in your own words why it is important for a judge to be independent and not influenced by other people.

ROUGH JUSTICE

Today we have judges to help protect our freedom. If we are accused of a crime, we might be judged in a trial. But it hasn't always been this way.

Over 1000 years ago, back in Anglo-Saxon times, the Anglo-Saxons used to decide whether someone was guilty of a crime by using 'ordeals'. An ordeal is an unpleasant trial. By putting people through an ordeal, they believed that God would decide if they were guilty.

One ordeal involved the person accused of the crime being forced to plunge their hand into a barrel of boiling water to grab a stone from the bottom. If, after three days, the blistered hand was infected (which was highly likely) then the person was declared guilty. If found guilty, they might have a hand or nose or perhaps an ear chopped off as punishment. Or they might even be hanged.

Because the Anglo-Saxons did not have prisons, these brutal punishments were intended to put people off committing crimes in the first place. We call this a deterrent.

Until about 150 years ago, people accused of crimes were put in the stocks and pelted with rotten fruit, or those unable to pay their rent might be thrown into prison. In those days, the poorer you were, the more likely it was you would be punished, since the well-off could often afford to pay their way out of trouble. Today, everyone – rich and poor – is treated equally by the law.

What we mean when we say...

Anglo-Saxons: tribes from Germany, Holland and Denmark who lived in Britain from around 410 to 1066 AD.

Trial: a formal examination of evidence, usually in front of a jury, in order to decide whether someone is guilty.

Accuse: claim that someone has done something wrong.

Prison: a building used to lock away people who have been convicted of committing crimes.

Deterrent: something that discourages you from doing something. For example, prison is a deterrent to people stealing.

Your turn to speak

Punishments act as deterrents. Can you think of any punishments that stop you from breaking a rule at school or at home?

Read and understand

1. Draw your own picture of an Anglo-Saxon ordeal.

2. Explain why the Anglo-Saxons used such harsh punishments. Why don't we use these today?

WHERE LAWS COME FROM

The Law of the Land has been developed over hundreds of years and a lot of laws are even older than Parliament itself.

Some laws have been around for hundreds of years, whilst new laws have been created recently to cope with new situations. For example, laws about speeding limits of 70 miles per hour would not have made any sense before the invention of motor cars.

Our earliest laws date back to the King's Bench, a system set up by the King of England who ruled after 1066, or even earlier. The King sat on a bench in the Palace of Westminster where he heard disputes and dispensed justice. After a while though, the King tired of listening to all those complaints, so he appointed judges to settle arguments on his behalf.

Many laws were different in different parts of the country. This was confusing, so the King told the most important judges to try to make the law the same for everyone, wherever they lived.

Later judges looked back on past customs and decisions to help them decide the law. Laws based on past decisions are known as *Common Law*.

What we mean when we say...

Law of the Land: all of the laws in a country.

King's Bench: a court where the King heard and settled disputes.

Common Law: laws based on customs and earlier legal decisions.

Your turn to speak

Discuss with your partner:

→ Imagine you are the King deciding how to settle an argument – a man comes to your court saying that he owns a flock of sheep, but that a local Lord has stolen his flock. The Lord says the flock of sheep belongs to him. How would you decide who is telling the truth and who the flock of sheep belongs to?

→ Why do you think it is a good idea that the Law of the Land should be the same for everyone throughout the country? What problems might there be if laws were different in different parts of the country?

Read and understand

1. Draw a picture of the King sitting on the King's Bench settling arguments. The King will probably be surrounded by his lords, with a long queue of people waiting for the King to decide how their problem should be sorted out and to dispense justice.

2. What was the King's Bench?

3. Why did the King ask judges to make the law the same in all parts of the country?

4. Describe what we mean by Common Law.

ACTS OF PARLIAMENT

New laws are created by Acts of Parliament or Statutes or Legislation.

Most new laws are put forward by the Government, although sometimes a Member of Parliament will have an idea for a new law.

Potential new laws are known as Bills. Bills are debated by Members of Parliament (MPs) and are then talked about in more detail by small committees of MPs.

Parliament is made up of the House of Commons, with its 650 elected MPs, and the House of Lords. When a Bill has been approved by both the House of Commons and the House of Lords, it is passed to the Monarch for final approval, known as the Royal Assent.

Once a Bill has received the Royal Assent, it is called an Act of Parliament and becomes part of the Law of the Land.

What we mean when we say...

Government: the group of people that we have chosen to run our country.

Act of Parliament: an action that creates a new law.

Bill: a potential law that has been suggested for discussion in Parliament.

Royal Assent: when the Monarch gives approval for a new law.

Your turn to speak

Quick test with your partner. Test each other on the meaning of the following:

→ What is an Act of Parliament?

→ What is a Bill?

→ Who has to give a Bill final approval?

→ What is the name we use for a Bill's final approval?

Read and understand

1. Imagine the Monarch (King or Queen) giving their approval or Royal Assent to a Bill so that it becomes an act of Parliament. Hundreds of years ago, the Monarch used to do this in person. Draw a picture of the Monarch giving their Royal Assent.

2. Who puts forward suggestions for new laws?

3. Describe what happens to a Bill before it becomes a new law.

4. What new law would you like to put forward to Parliament?

THE RULE OF LAW

Here are six rules which help us tell whether laws are good or bad, and whether the legal system is working correctly or not. Together, these rules form the Rule of Law.

The Rule of Law means that:

1. Everyone should know what laws they need to obey.
2. Laws should be the same for everyone.
3. We should always use laws, not just our own opinion of what seems right or wrong, to decide if someone has broken the law.
4. Judges, the police and members of the Government must always use their powers fairly.
5. Everyone accused of breaking the law should have a fair trial. They should be treated as 'innocent until proved guilty'.
6. Laws should always try to protect everyone's Human Rights.

If all of these rules are being followed, you can be pretty sure that the Rule of Law is working well.

What we mean when we say...

The Rule of Law: a set of rules that help us tell whether laws are good or bad and whether the legal system is working properly.

Human Rights: privileges everybody should have because they are human.

Your turn to speak

Discuss with your partner:

→ What would happen to the law if the police, the Government or judges did not use their powers fairly?

→ Why do you think that everyone accused of a crime should have a fair trial?

→ The law says that anyone accused of a crime should be treated as if they are 'innocent until proved guilty'. What do you think this means?

Read and understand

1. Make a 'Rule of Law' poster showing the six rules that help us tell if the Rule of Law is working properly.

2. Look at the six rules. Which do you think is the most important? Explain why.

3. Describe in your own words what you think we mean by the Rule of Law.

CRIMINAL LAW

Britain's legal system is split into two halves. One half deals with Criminal Law, and the other half deals with Civil Law.

Criminal Law deals with crime and punishment. Criminal Law's main job is to keep us safe.

Civil Law sets out rules for how society is organised and helps to sort out arguments between people.

Criminal Law deals with crimes like robbery, and keeps us safe by punishing people who break the law (commit a crime). The less crime a society has to put up with, the happier and fairer it will be for everyone.

Have a look at Nick here. Nick is busy being a very naughty boy, stealing sweets from a shop. Now we can't blame Nick for wanting sweets. But we can blame him for taking sweets that are not his and that he hasn't paid for. Nick is breaking the Law of the Land by committing a criminal offence: theft. Theft is a threat to a happy, fair society.

Bobbies on the beat: the police and prosecution

Crimes are investigated by the police who collect evidence from crime scenes.

Evidence is something that can be used to prove somebody's guilt in court. Evidence might be fingerprints or perhaps a statement from an eyewitness.

The Crown Prosecution Service (or CPS for short) decides if the police have collected enough evidence to prosecute the suspect; this is the person that the police think might have committed the crime. To prosecute means to take somebody to court and put them on trial where they will be officially accused of a crime.

For a court to find someone guilty, they have to be absolutely 100% sure that the suspect committed the crime. Suspects are 'innocent until proved guilty', not the other way round.

If a person is convicted (found guilty), Criminal Law can punish them in a number of ways:
+ Prison. This is to punish the criminal and deter people from committing crimes in the future.
+ Paying a fine: having to pay money. This might be to the victim of their crime.
+ Community service. The criminal is sometimes made to do work which will benefit other people.

What we mean when we say...

Criminal Law: deals with crime and punishment. Criminal Law keeps us safe.

Civil Law: sets out the rules for society and helps sort out arguments between people.

Crown Prosecution Service: the part of the Government that decides whether there is enough evidence to prosecute someone.

Evidence: facts or information that help us tell if something is true.

Eyewitness: a person who has seen or heard something happen and can describe it.

Investigate: carefully examine the facts in order to establish the truth.

Prosecute: take someone to court and accuse them of a crime.

Suspect: the person accused of committing a crime.

Convicted: found guilty.

Your turn to speak

Discuss with your partner:

→ What does Criminal Law do? What kind of crimes does it deal with?

→ What kind of evidence can you think of that the police might collect to help prove whether a suspect has committed a crime?

→ What kind of punishments might be given to someone convicted of a crime?

Read and understand

1. Draw a poster showing the different kinds of evidence that the police might collect when investigating a crime. Try taking your own fingerprints.

2. Whose job is it to decide if the police have collected enough evidence for a suspect to be prosecuted?

3. Why do you think that people convicted of crimes are given punishments?

BOUNDARY ISSUES:
CIVIL LAW

The other half of our legal system is Civil Law.

Civil Law deals with more or less everything that isn't a crime. It helps organise our society and sort out arguments like:
→   Who owns what.
→   Who can work for whom.
→   Who can build what, and where.
→   Who can sell what, and to whom.
→   Family matters such as marriage and divorce.

Civil Law is used to sort out arguments between people. For example, Michael and Jenny are having an argument about where Michael's garden finishes and Jenny's garden begins.

The fence has fallen down and Michael has drawn his own boundary, making his garden much bigger than Jenny's. This isn't fair on Jenny at all.

Luckily, Jenny has Civil Law to help her out.

Jenny cannot call the police, because Michael isn't committing a criminal offence by painting his own boundary. But what she can do is sue him. Suing someone means taking them to a civil court and trying to prove that they have wronged you.

What we mean when we say...

Sue: to take someone to court to prove they have wronged you.

Your turn to speak

→ Make a list with your partner of the kind of issues that would be dealt with by Civil Law.

→ Pretend you are having a dispute (argument) with your partner. It might be similar to the one Michael and Jenny were having. Take it in turns to say why you think you are right and your partner is wrong.

Read and understand

1. Make a poster showing the type of problems that Civil Law will help sort out.

2. Describe what happens when you sue someone.

3. What problems do you think there might be if we did not have laws to help sort out arguments between people?

4. Make a leaflet showing that there are two halves of the law – Criminal Law and Civil Law. Show in your leaflet the kinds of crime or problem that each half of the law deals with.

DO YOU REMEMBER?

Let's finish by reminding ourselves of some of the most important points we've learned:

→ Laws are just like the rules you have at home and at school. We have rules and laws for everyone's benefit; to help keep our lives safe, fair and organised.

→ You are responsible for your own behaviour, and should always try to act fairly and respectfully towards others – whether you like them or not!

→ Living under the Law of the Land protects our individual liberty, our equality and our democracy.

→ We have a judiciary to look after the country's legal system. The judiciary is made up of judges who interpret and apply laws within the court system.

→ We use a system called Parliamentary democracy to elect MPs to represent our views and make our laws in the House of Commons.

→ The judiciary is an independent part of the Government. Judicial independence tries to make sure that our justice system is objective and fair.

→ Our justice system has developed over hundreds of years, and is still developing today.

→ New laws are created by Acts of Parliament.

→ Criminal Law deals with crime and punishment.

→ Civil Law deals with disputes between people.